Classic Rock of the Late '60s

The Woodstock Era

'50s EARLY R&B | '50s ROCK 'N' ROLL | '60s BRITISH INVASION | '70s CLASSIC ROCK ERA | '80s PROG/GLAM/VIDEO | '90s HEAVY ROCK

'50s DOO-WOP | '60s AMERICAN POP | '60s WOODSTOCK | '80s PUNK/NEW WAVE/METAL | '90s ALT/UNPLUGGED

Project Manager: AARON STANG
Design & Art Layout: LISA GREENE MANE
Foreword: JEFFREY PEPPER RODGERS
Cover Photo: CORBIS
Interior photos courtesy of STAR FILE INC.

Artist Index

Contents

Foreword

Perhaps more than any time before or since, the chaotic, colorful years of the late '60s were brilliantly captured—and even inspired—by the music. From the hippie flowering and the drug culture to the struggles over civil rights and the Vietnam War, rock 'n' roll was on the scene, rallying the baby-boom generation as well as capturing its divisions in stark relief. New human experiences call for new sounds to express them, and these years saw an extraordinary surge of invention, exploration, and upheaval throughout American society.

Crosby, Stills, Nash & Young

Creedence Clearwater Revival

In these pages are many examples of songs that defined their historical and cultural moment. The iconic 1969 gathering of the hippie tribes in upstate New York for "three days of peace and music" found its classic expression in Joni Mitchell's dreamy "Woodstock," which her friends Crosby, Stills, Nash & Young turned into a driving rock anthem (ironically, Mitchell never even made it to the festival—she was waylaid in a hotel and following it on TV). Out on the other coast, the Grateful Dead provided an essential soundtrack for the psychedelic experience, from folk-based songs like "Uncle John's Band" to wildly unconventional and open-ended concert journeys like "Dark Star"—a sound and style that would have been unimaginable just a few years earlier.

The Woodstock generation certainly did not all march to the same drummer. Never ones to follow Scott Mackenzie's advice to San Francisco pilgrims to "wear some flowers in your hair," John Fogerty and Creedence Clearwater Revival brought a distinctly un-hippie-like fire and focus to rock 'n' roll, from joyful melodies like "Proud Mary" and "Down on the Corner" to the working-class salvo "Fortunate Son." While part of the counterculture favored hedonism over politics, some young artists walked right into the fray—notably a precocious 15-year-old named Janis Ian, whose song "Society's Child," a portrait of interracial romance, struck a nerve and created a furor.

Several of these songs come from the fusion of folk and rock, which helped raise the bar of the music's ambitions and elevate the image of its practitioners from entertainers into artists. Over in England, Steve Winwood and Traffic paid tribute to the traditional ballad form in "John Barleycorn" even while exploring the long, loose jam in songs like "Dear Mr. Fantasy." Roger McGuinn, originally a banjo and 12-string guitar picker from the Chicago folk scene, dipped into the influential Pete Seeger songbook for "Turn! Turn! Turn!" for his new electric band the Byrds, whose jingle-jangle still rings through roots rock today. And wherever this music traveled, the blues went hand in hand, as can be traced here through Eric Clapton's searing guitar with Derek and the Dominoes, Blind Faith, and the psychedelic power-trio Cream.

Whether or not you were actually there at the be-in, the acid test, or the burning of draft cards or bras, this music remains as evocative as ever, a witness to a time when America catapulted into a new era.

Jeffrey Pepper Rodgers

Courtesy of IRV STEINBERG/STAR FILE INC.

The Byrds

Eric Clapton

Courtesy of BARRIE WENTZELL/STAR FILE INC.

Courtesy of JEFF MAYER/STAR FILE INC.

Grateful Dead

Courtesy of ROBERTO RABANNE/STAR FILE INC.

Joni Mitchell

Courtesy of DAGMAR/STAR FILE INC.

Van Morrison

BELL BOTTOM BLUES

Words and Music by
ERIC CLAPTON

Bell Bottom Blues - 9 - 1

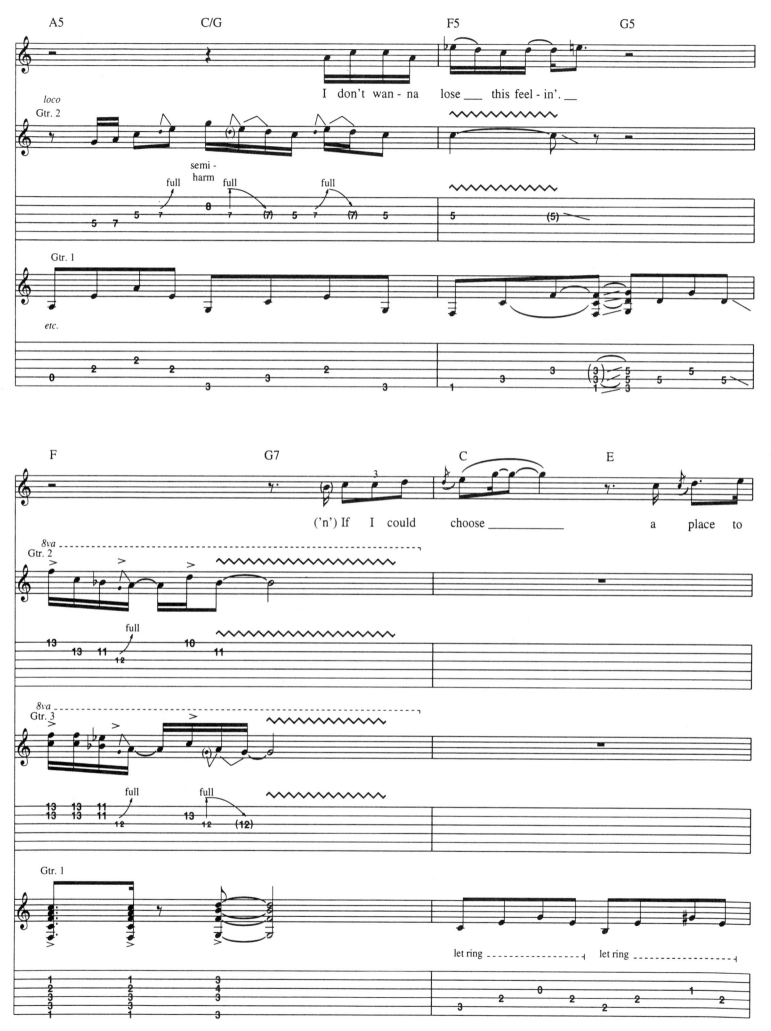

Bell Bottom Blues - 9 - 2

12

14

16

* Pinched mute w/thumb of of R.H. - producing semi-harmonics.

18

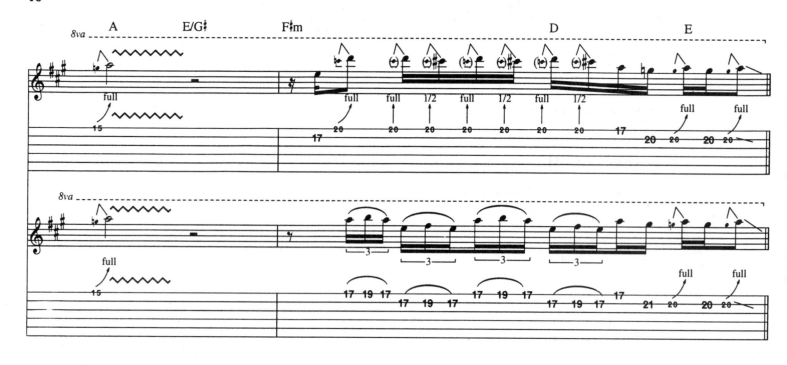

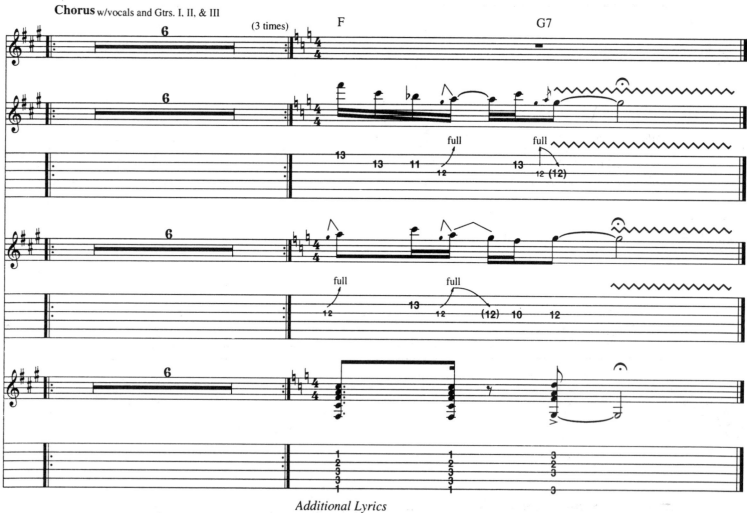

Additional Lyrics

2. It's all wrong, but it's all right
   The way that you treat me baby.
   Once I was strong but I lost the fight;
   You won't find a better loser. *(To Pre-chorus, then Chorus)*

3. Bell Bottom Blues, don't say "Goodbye."
   We're surely gonna meet again.
   And if we do don't ya be surprised.
   If you find me with another lover. *(To Pre-chorus, then Chorus)*

BIG YELLOW TAXI

Gtr. tuning:
⑥ = E ③ = G#
⑤ = B ② = B
④ = E ① = E

Words and Music by
JONI MITCHELL

Moderately fast ♩ = 172

Intro:

Gtr. 1

1.They paved par-a-dise, put up a park-ing lot,—
2.3.4. See additional lyrics

with a pink ho - tel,— a

bou - tique, and a swing - ing hot__ spot.__

20

Verse 2:
They took all the trees,
Put them in a tree museum.
And they charged all the people
A dollar and a half just to see 'em.
(To Chorus:)

Verse 3:
Hey farmer, farmer,
Put away the D.D.T., now.
Give me spots on all my apples,
But leave me the birds and the bees.
Please!
(To Chorus:)

Verse 4:
Late last night,
I heard the screen door slam,
And a big yellow taxi
Took away my old man.
(To Chorus:)

BORN TO BE WILD

Words and Music by
MARS BONFIRE

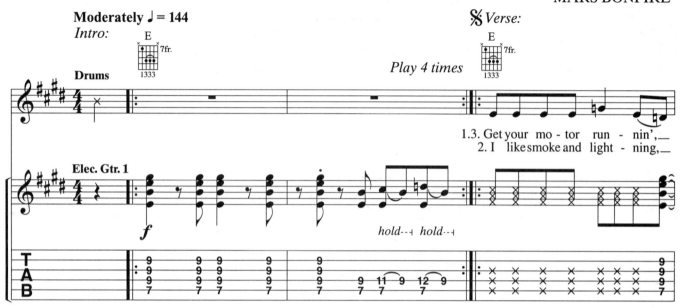

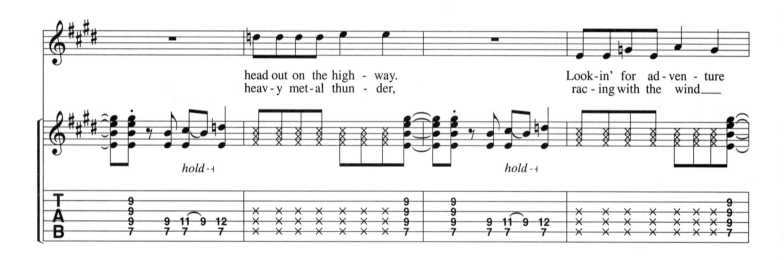

Born to Be Wild - 4 - 4

BROWN EYED GIRL

Words and Music by
VAN MORRISON

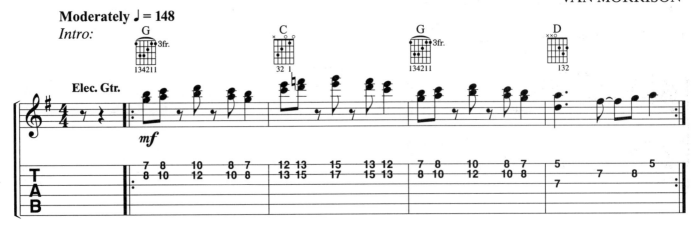

*Elec. Gtr. simile on repeats.

Brown Eyed Girl - 4 - 1

Brown Eyed Girl - 4 - 2

HEY, TONIGHT

Words and Music by
J. C. FOGERTY

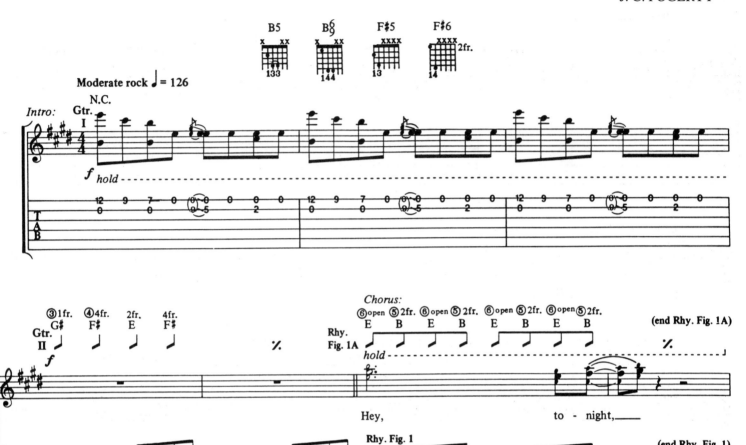

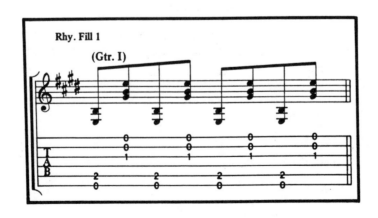

Hey, Tonight - 3 - 1

Hey, Tonight - 3 - 2

CAN'T FIND MY WAY HOME

Words and Music by
STEVE WINWOOD

Can't Find My Way Home - 13 - 1

34

Come

Can't Find My Way Home - 13 - 2

Can't Find My Way Home - 13 - 5

Can't Find My Way Home - 13 - 6

42

Can't Find My Way Home - 13 - 11

Can't Find My Way Home - 13 - 12

Can't Find My Way Home - 13 - 13

CALIFORNIA DREAMIN'

Words and Music by
JOHN PHILLIPS and MICHELLE PHILLIPS

California Dreamin' - 2 - 1

dream-in'
(Cal - i - for - nia dream - in' on such a win-ter's day._____)

2. Stopped in - to a church,__

Flute Solo:

Cont. rhy. simile

D.S. 𝄊 al Coda

3. All the leaves are

Coda

dream-in'
(Cal - i - for - nia dream - in' on such a win-ter's, Cal - i - for - nia dream-

6-str. & 12-str. Acous. Gtrs.

___ On such a win - ter's day_____ On such a win-ter's day._____
- in' on such a win-ter's, Cal - i - for - nia dream - in' on such a win-ter's day._____)

Verse 2:
Stopped into a church
I passed along the way.
Well, I got down on my knees (Got down on my knees.)
And I pretend to pray. (I pretend to pray.)
You know the preacher liked the cold (Preacher liked the cold.)
He knows I'm gonna stay. (Knows I'm gonna stay.)
(To Chorus:)

Verse 3:
All the leaves are brown (All the leaves are brown)
And the sky is gray. (And the sky is gray.)
I've been for a walk (I've been for a walk)
On a winter's day. (On a winter's day.)
If I didn't tell her, (If I didn't tell her,)
I could leave today. (I could leave today.)
(To Chorus:)

CREEQUE ALLEY

Words and Music by
JOHN PHILLIPS and MICHELLE GILLIAM

1. John and Mit - chie were get - tin' kind of itch - y just to leave the folk mu - sic be - hind.

2.3.4.6. See additional lyrics
5. Flute solo

Zal and Den - ny, work - in' for a pen - ny, try'n'

to get a fish on the line. In a cof - fee house Se - bas - tian sat,

and af - ter ev - 'ry num - ber they passed the hat. Mc-

Guinn and Mc - Guire's just a - get - tin' high - er in L. A., you know where that's at.

And no__ one's get-tin' fat ex-cept Ma-ma Cass.__

Outro:

Verse 2:
Zally said, "Denny, you know there aren't many
Who can sing a song the way that you do."
"Let's go south." Denny said, "Zally, golly, don't you think that
I wish I could play guitar like you?"
Zal, Denny, and Sebastian sat, (at the Night Owl)
And after every number they passed the hat.
McGuinn and McGuire still are gettin' higher in L. A.,
You know where that's at.
And no one's gettin' fat except Mama Cass.

Verse 3:
When Cass was a sophomore, planned to go to Swarthmore,
But she changed her mind one day.
Standin' on the turnpike, thumb out to hitchhike,
Take her to New York right away.
When Denny met Cass, he gave her love bumps,
Called John and Zal and that was the Mugwumps.
McGuinn and McGuire couldn't get no higher
But that's what they were aimin' at.
And no one's gettin' fat except Mama Cass.

Verse 4:
Mugwumps, high jumps, low slumps, big bumps,
Don't you work as hard as you play?
Make-up, break-up, everything you shake up,
Guess it had to be that way.
Sebastian and Zal formed the Spoonful,
Michelle, John, and Denny gettin' very tuneful.
McGuinn and McGuire, just a-catchin' fire in L.A.,
You know where that's at.
And everybody's gettin' fat except Mama Cass.
(To Flute Solo:)

Verse 6:
Broke, busted, disgusted, agents can't be trusted,
And then she wants to go to the sea.
Cass can't make it, she says, "We'll have to fake it."
We knew she'd come eventually.
Greasin' on American Express cards, tents, low rent,
But keepin' out the heat's hard.
Duffy's good vibrations and our imaginations
Can't go on indefinitely.
And California dreamin' is becoming a reality.

DARK STAR

Words by ROBERT HUNTER
Music by JERRY GARCIA, MICKEY HART,
BILL KREUTZMANN, PHIL LESH,
RON McKERNAN and BOB WEIR

Dark Star - 4 - 1

Dark Star - 4 - 2

52

Dark Star - 4 - 3

*Two gtrs. arranged as one.

**Bass arranged w/gtrs.

*Two gtrs. arranged as one.

Verse 2:
Mirror shatters in formless reflections of matter.
Glass hand dissolving to ice petal flowers revolving.
Lady in velvet recedes in the nights of good-bye...
(To Chorus:)

Dark Star - 4 - 4

DEAR MR. FANTASY

Words and Music by
STEVE WINWOOD, CHRIS WOOD
and JIM CAPALDI

Dear Mr. Fantasy - 15 - 1

some - thing   to make — us all — hap - py. _____

Do an-y-thing, — take — us — out of this — gloom. _____   Sing a song, —

— play gui - tar, _____   make it   snap - py. _____

Dear Mr. Fantasy - 15 - 2

Dear Mr. Fantasy - 15 - 4

58

60

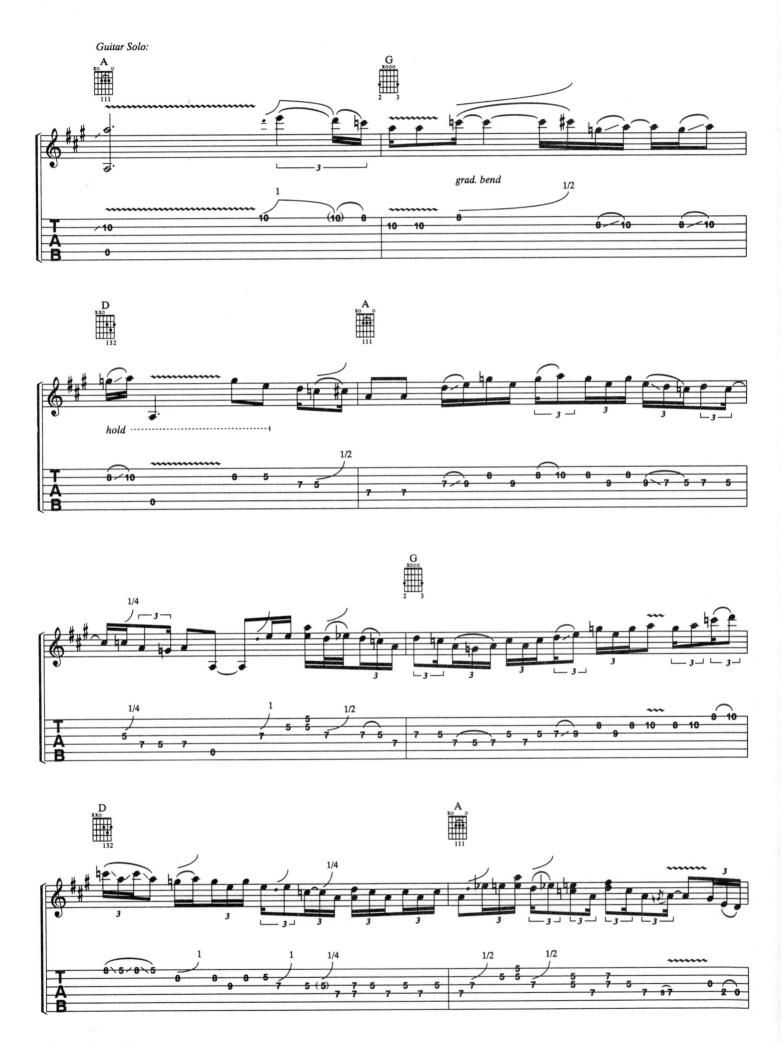

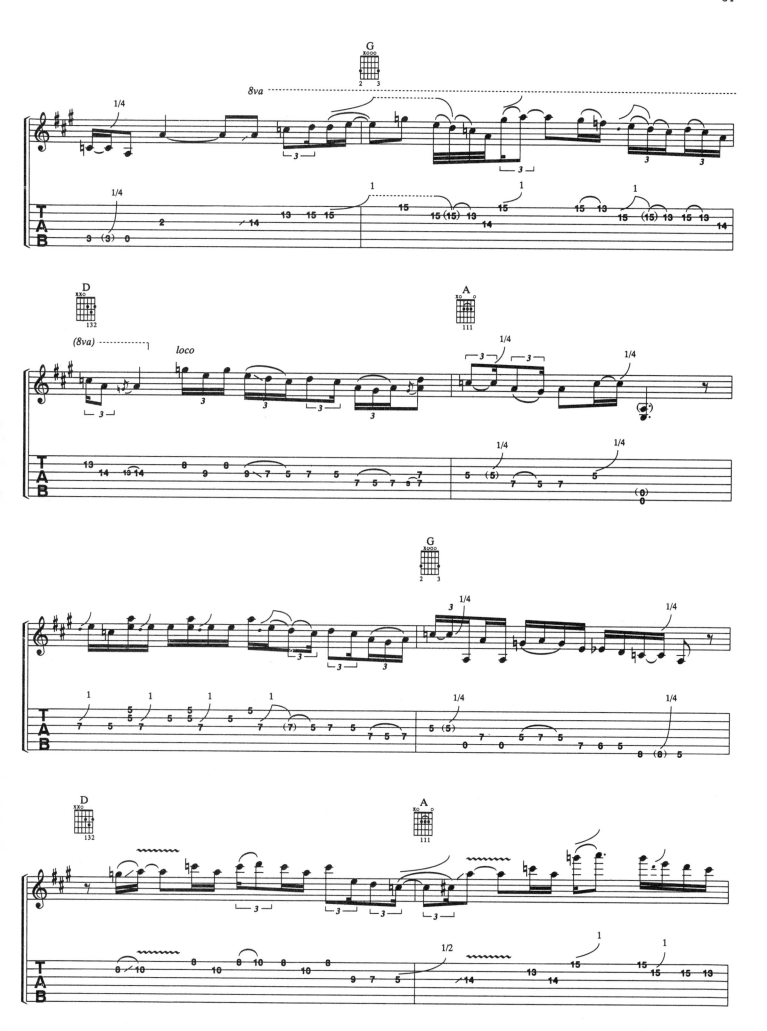

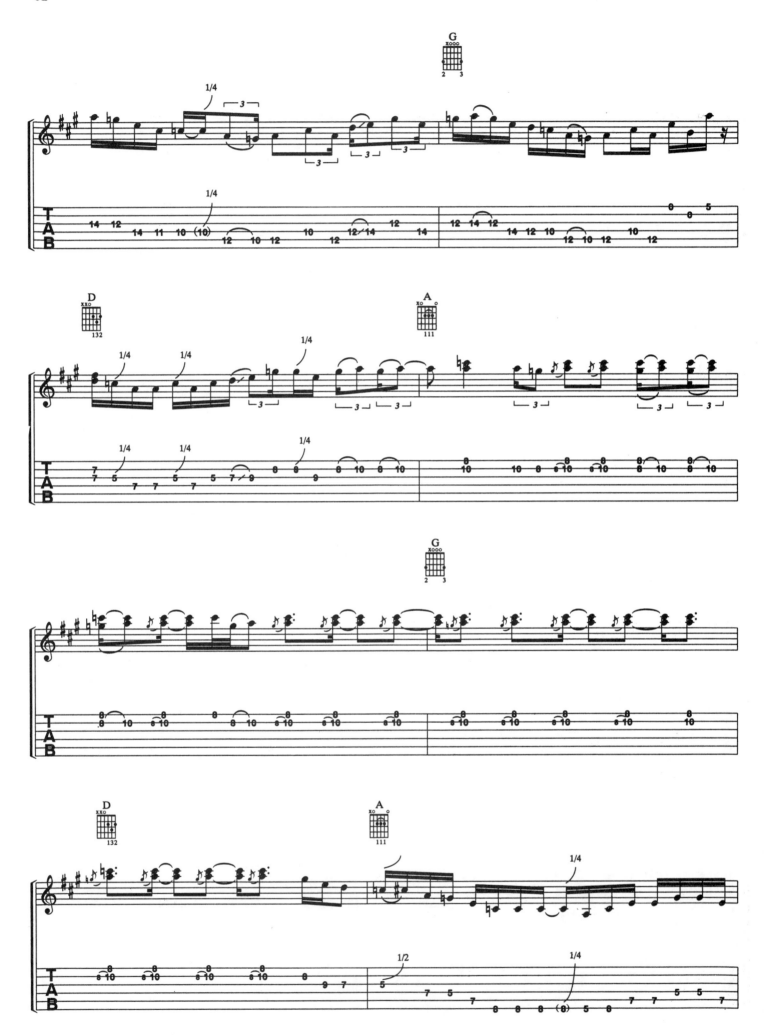

64

Dear Mr. Fantasy - 15 - 12

66

Dear Mr. Fantasy - 15 - 13

Dear Mr. Fantasy - 15 - 14

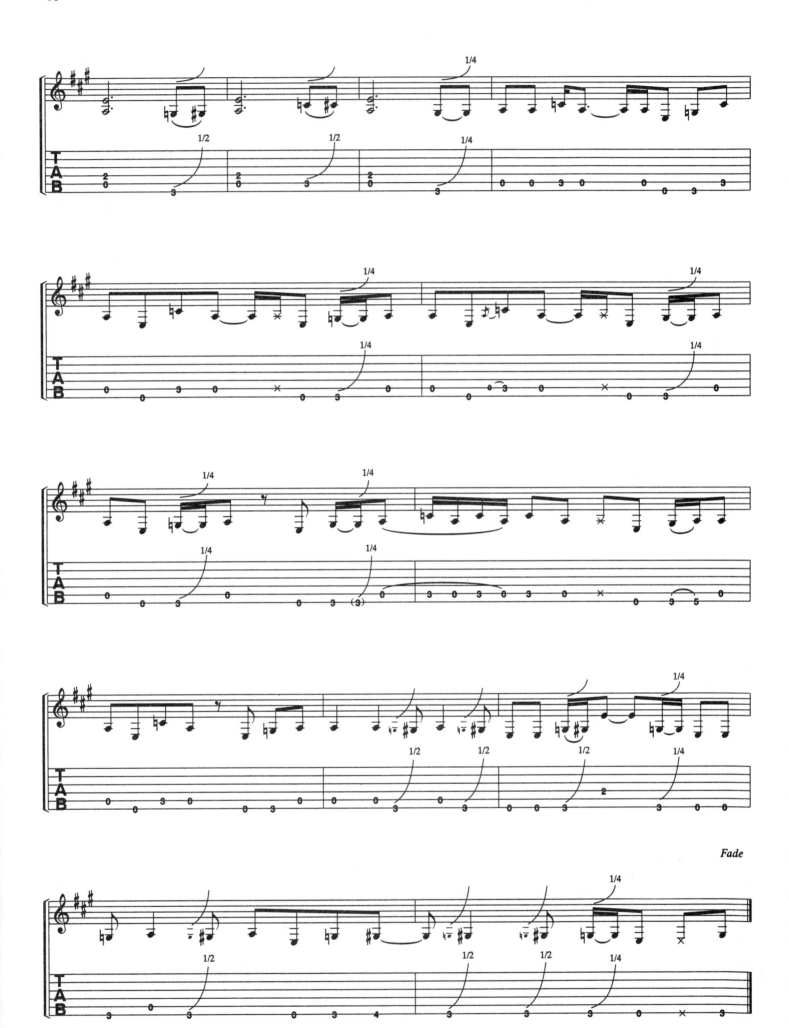

DEDICATED TO THE ONE I LOVE

Words and Music by
LOWMAN PAULING and RALPH BASS

DOWN ON THE CORNER

Words and Music by
JOHN C. FOGERTY

starting to un-wind._ Four kids on the cor - ner trying to bring you up; _

Chorus:

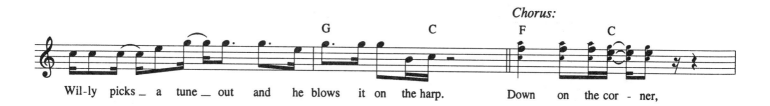

Wil-ly picks_ a tune_ out and he blows it on the harp. Down on the cor - ner,

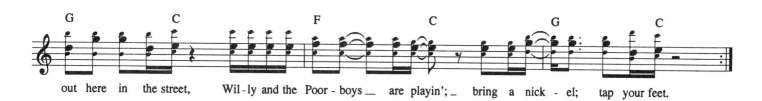

out here in the street, Wil-ly and the Poor-boys _ are playin';_ bring a nick - el; tap your feet.

Interlude:

Gtr. 2

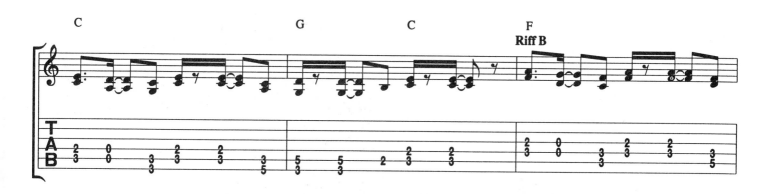

Down On The Corner – 3 – 2

74

FORTUNATE SON

By
J.C. FOGERTY

Fortunate Son - 5 - 1

C5   G5

ooh,   they point the can - non at you,   y'all.__

Chorus:
G5   D5   D5   C5

Rhy. Fig. 2

It ain't me,___   it ain't me;_____   I ain't no sen - a -tor's___ son.__

(end Rhy. Fig. 2)

G5   G   w/Rhy. Fig. 2   G5   D5

_ Y'all.__   It ain't me,___   it ain't me;_____

C5   G5

I ain't no for - tu -nate___ one,____   no.____

Fortunate Son - 5 - 2

78

Verse 3:
Some folks inherit star-spangled eyes.
Ooo, they send you down to war, y'all.
It ain't me.
It ain't me.
I'm no fortunate one, one.

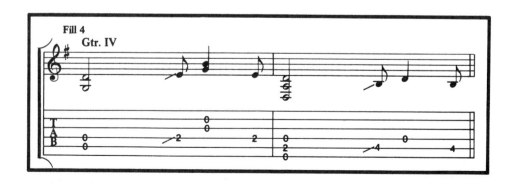

Fortunate Son - 5 - 5

EVIL WAYS

Words and Music by
SONNY HENRY

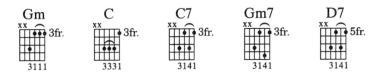

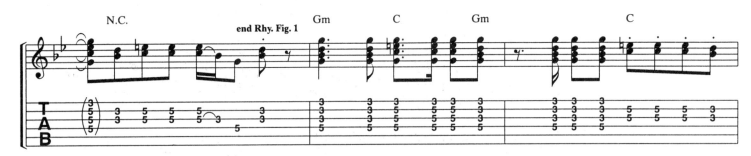

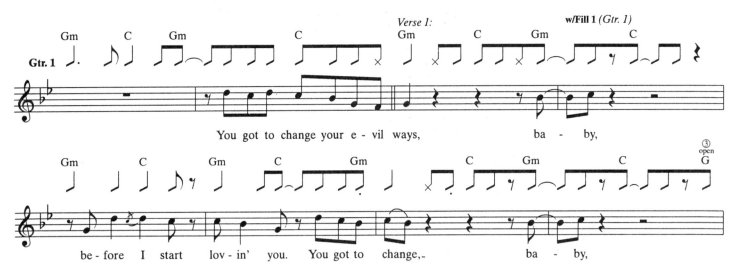

You got to change your e - vil ways, ba - by,

be - fore I start lov - in' you. You got to change,— ba - by,

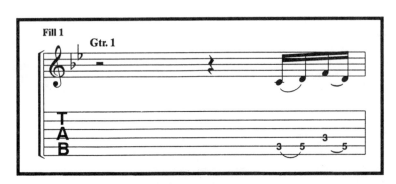

Evil Ways - 4 - 1

Evil Ways - 4 - 2

Evil Ways - 4 - 4

FOR WHAT IT'S WORTH

Buffalo Springfield's only big hit, "For What It's Worth" was written by Stephen Stills after witnessing the L.A.P.D.'s heavy-handedness at breaking up an anti-Vietnam student demonstration on Sunset Strip. Perhaps one of the mildest protest songs ever penned, "For What It's Worth" was immediately embraced by West Coast students as a 'peacenik' anthem, and on its release as a single, rocketed to number 7 in the U.S. charts. Its success caught Atlantic Records off-guard, and copies of Buffalo Springfield's first album were swiftly withdrawn and re-pressed to include the song.

Words and Music by
STEPHEN STILLS

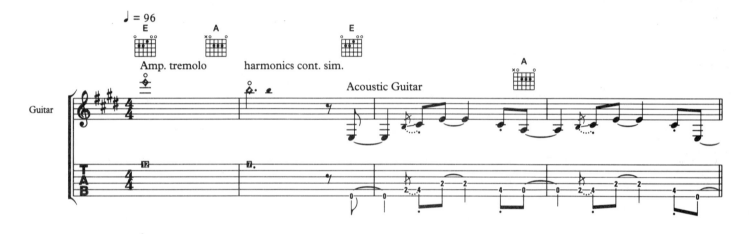

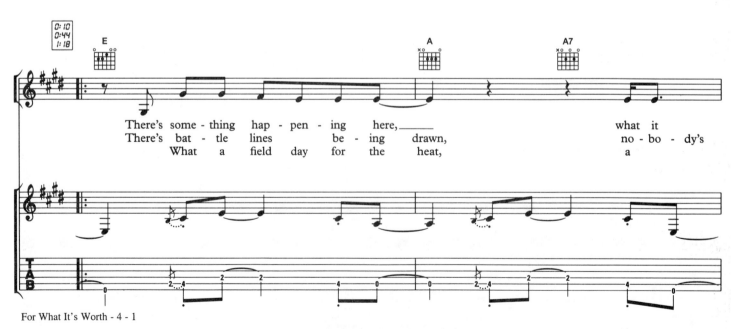

There's some-thing hap-pen-ing here, _____ what it
There's bat-tle lines be-ing drawn, no-bo-dy's
What a field day for the heat, a

For What It's Worth - 4 - 1

For What It's Worth - 4 - 2

86

For What It's Worth - 4 - 3

For What It's Worth - 4 - 4

HAVE YOU EVER SEEN THE RAIN?

By
J.C. FOGERTY

Have You Ever Seen the Rain? - 2 - 1

Verse 2:
Yesterday, and days before,
Sun is cold and rain is hard.
I know, been that way for all my time.

'Til forever, on it goes
Through the circle, fast and slow,
I know, and I can't stop. I wonder.

Have You Ever Seen The Rain? - 2 - 2

IN THE SUMMERTIME

Words and Music by
RAY DORSET

Verse:

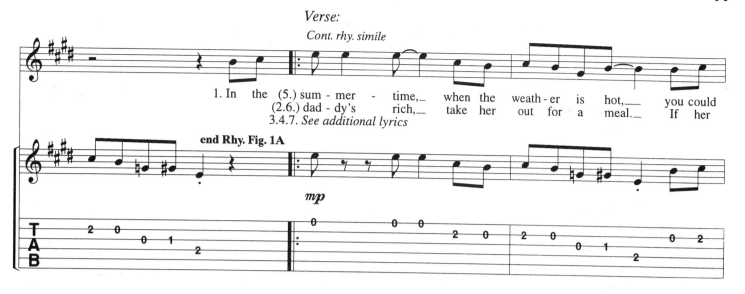

1. In the (5.) sum - mer - time,__ when the weath - er is hot,___ you could
(2.6.) dad - dy's rich,__ take her out for a meal.__ If her
3.4.7. *See additional lyrics*

stretch right up____ and__ touch__ the sky.__ When the weath - er is fine,__ you got
dad - dy's poor,__ and just__ do what you feel.__ Speed a - long the lane,__ do a

wom - en, you got wom - en on your mind.
turn or re - turn the twen - ty - five.

Have a drink, have a drive,
When the sun goes down, you can

In the Summertime - 4 - 3

Verses 3 & 7:
We're not bad people, we're not dirty, we're not mean.
We love everybody, but we do as we please.
When the weather is fine,
We go fishing or go swimming in the sea.
We're always happy,
Life's for living, yeah, that's our philosophy.

Verse 4:
When the winter's here, yeah, it's party time.
Bring your bottle the way you like
'Cause it'll soon be summertime.
When we see her again,
We'll go divin' on the reef,
We'll settle down.

In the Summertime - 4 - 4

IN-A-GADDA-DA-VIDA

Moderately ♩ = 108

Words and Music by
DOUG INGLE

*Elec. Gtr. 2 enters 2nd time.

Verse:
w/Riff A (Elec. Gtr. 1) 4 times
w/Rhy. Fig. 1 (Elec. Gtr. 2) 4 times

In - a-gad-da-da-vi - da, hon - ey, don't you know that I love____ you?____

In - a-gad-da-da-vi - da, ba - by, don't you know that I'll al - ways be true?____

LAYLA

Words and Music by
ERIC CLAPTON and JIM GORDON

Layla – 9 – 1

98

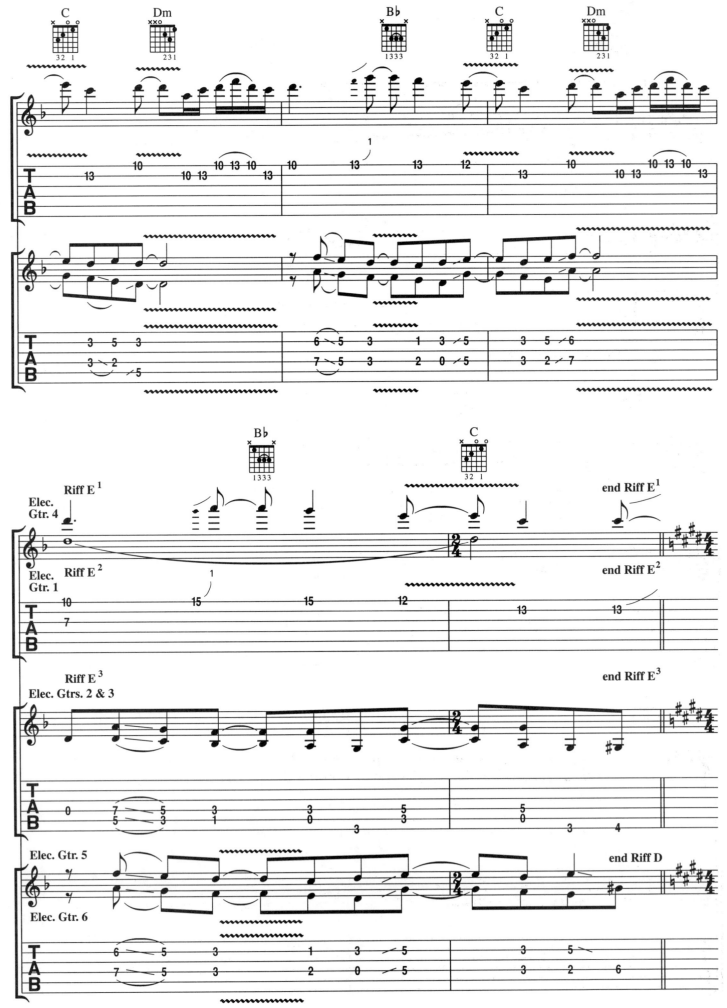

Layla – 9 – 2

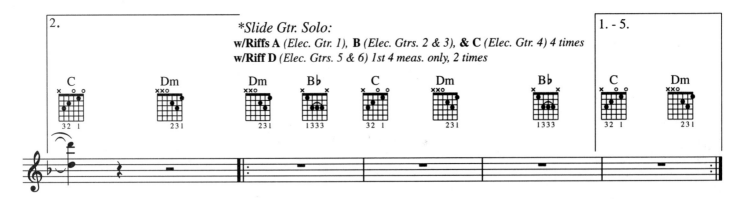

*w/ad lib. slide gtr. solo (D minor pentatonic scale).

*Elec. Gtr. is a composite gtr. combining piano and elec. gtrs.

Layla – 9 – 7

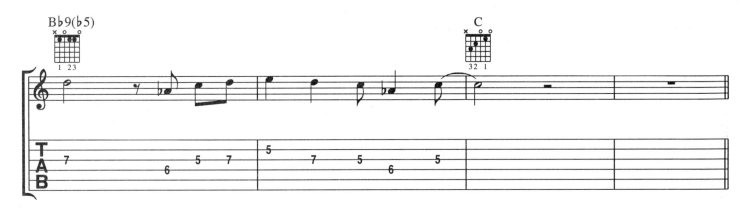

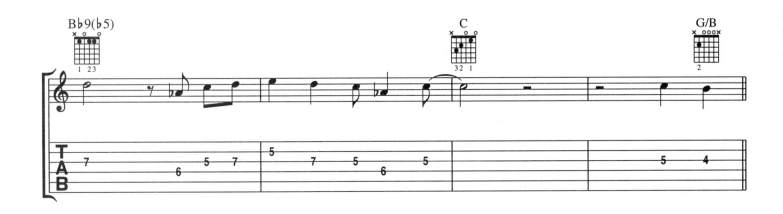

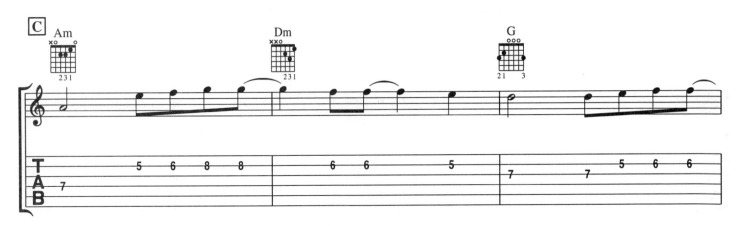

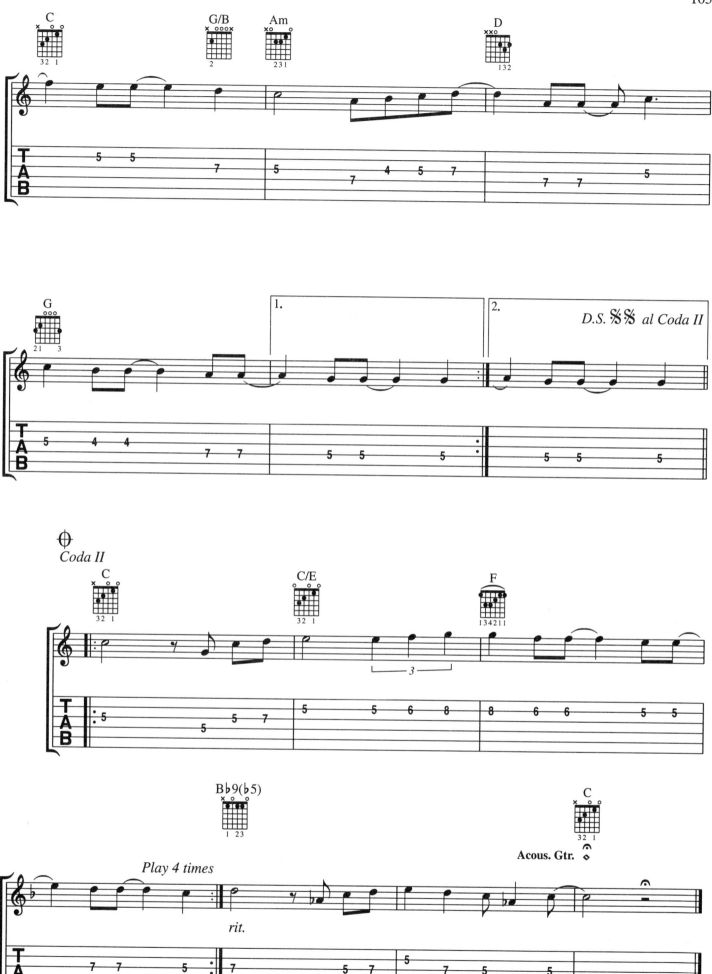

Layla – 9 – 9

JOHN BARLEYCORN
(Must Die)

Words and Music by
STEVE WINWOOD

John Barleycorn - 6 - 2

108

John Barleycorn - 6 - 3

John Barleycorn - 6 - 4

110

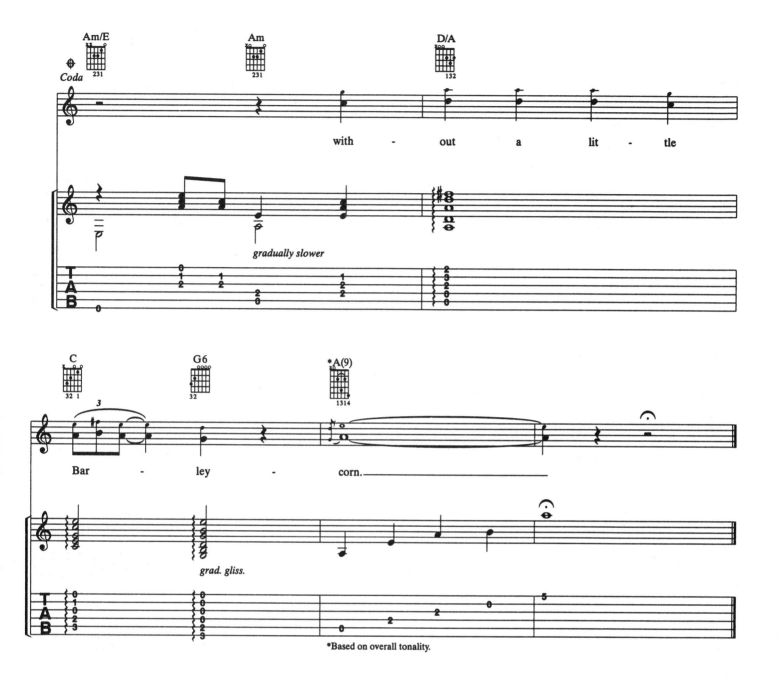

Verse 4:
They've wheeled him around and around the field
Till they came unto a barn.
And there they made a solemn oath
On poor John Barleycorn.
They've hired men with the crabtree sticks
To cut him skin from bone.
And the miller, he has served him worse than that,
For he's ground him between two stones.
(To Flute Solo:)

Verse 5:
And little Sir John and his nut-round bowl
And his brandy in the glass.
And little Sir John and his nut-round bowl
Proved the strongest man at last.
The huntsmen, he cut off the fox,
More so loudly to blow his horn.
And the tinker, he can't mend kettle nor pot
Without a little Barleycorn.

MACARTHUR PARK

Words and Music by
JIMMY WEBB

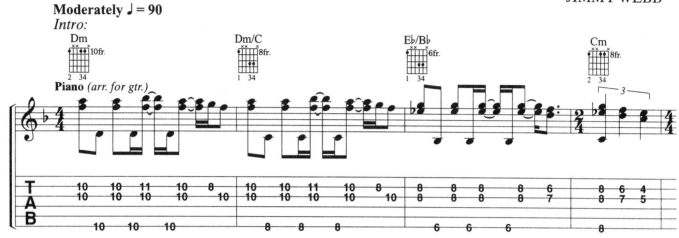

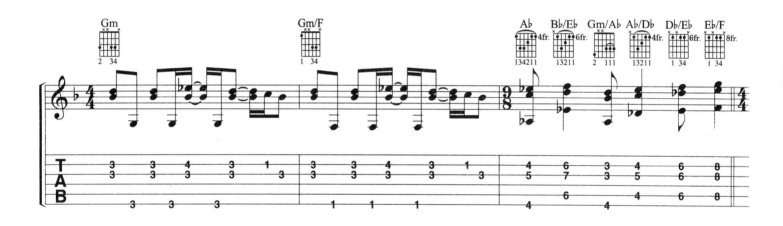

MacArthur Park - 6 - 1

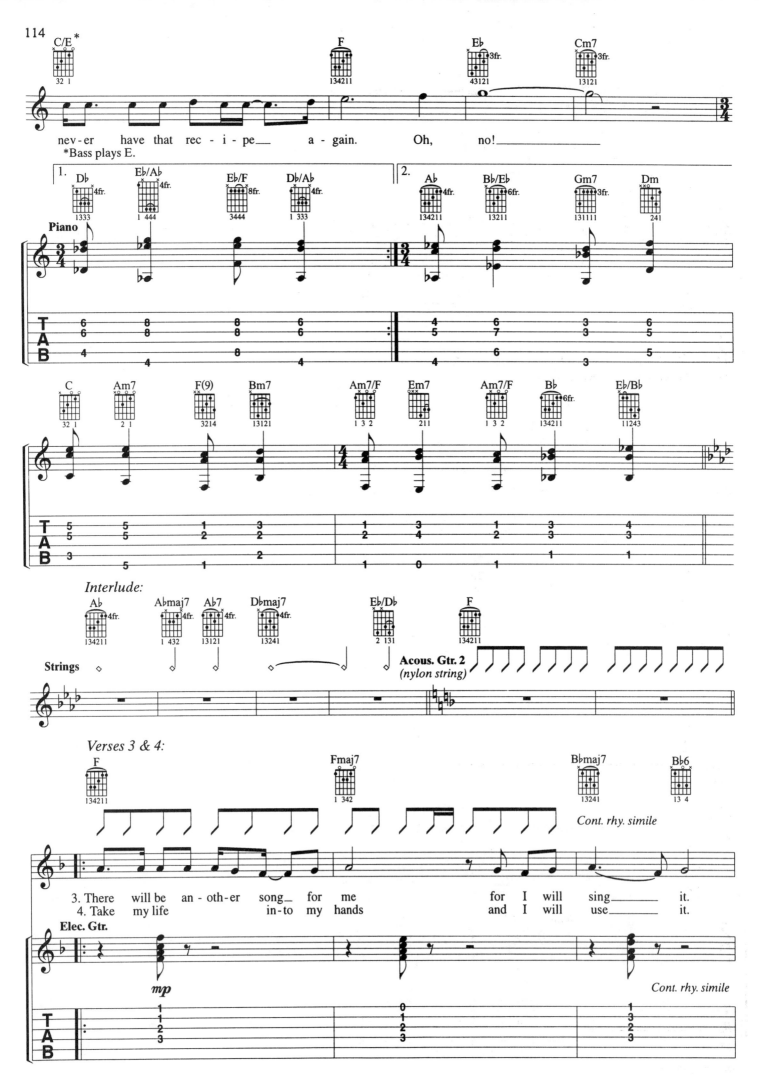

nev-er have that rec-i-pe___ a-gain. Oh, no!_____
*Bass plays E.

Piano

Interlude:

Strings

Acous. Gtr. 2
(nylon string)

Verses 3 & 4:

Cont. rhy. simile

3. There will be an-oth-er song___ for me   for I will sing_____ it.
4. Take my life in-to my hands   and I will use_____ it.

Elec. Gtr.

mp

Cont. rhy. simile

Double time

Instrumental Interlude:

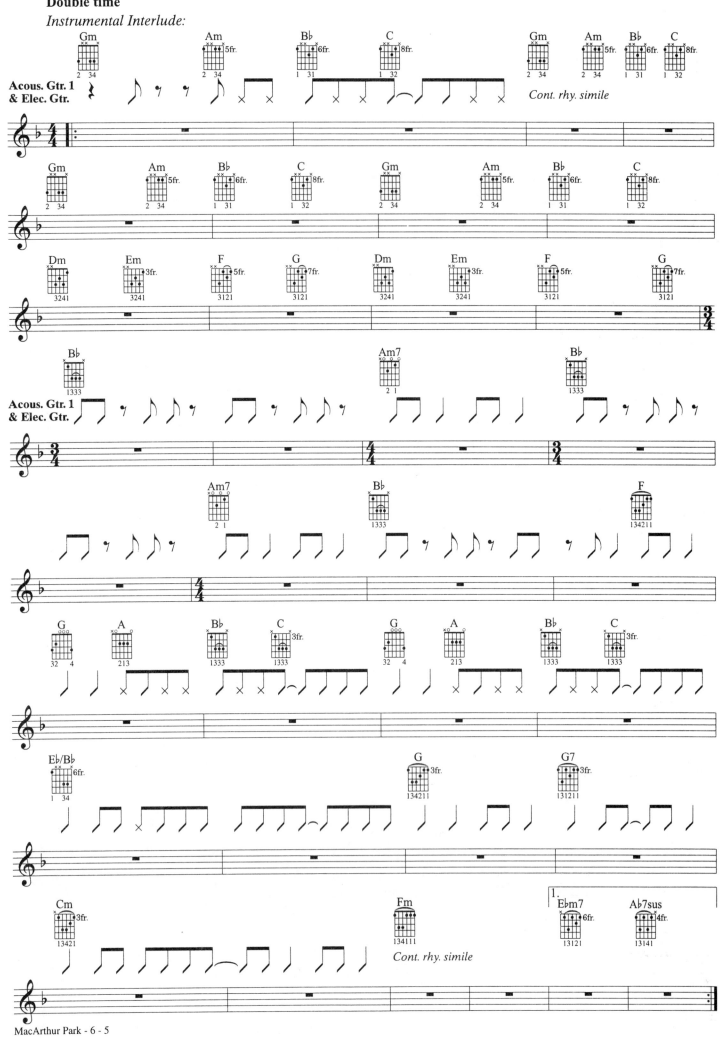

MAGIC CARPET RIDE

Words and Music by
RUSHTON MOREVE and JOHN KAY

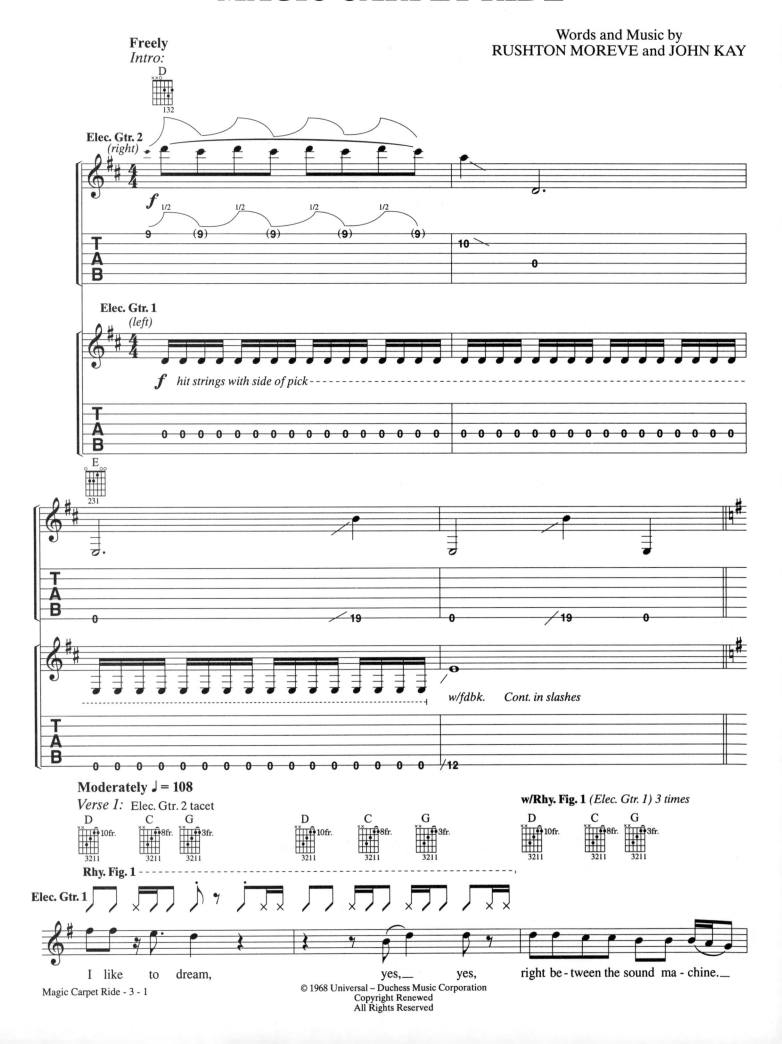

I like to dream,   yes,___ yes,   right be - tween the sound ma - chine.___

Magic Carpet Ride - 3 - 1

Magic Carpet Ride - 3 - 2

Verse 2:

w/Rhy. Fig. 1 *(Elec. Gtr. 1) 3 times*

night I held A - lad - din's lamp,__ and so I wished that I could stay.

Be - fore the thing could an - swer me, well, some - one came and took the lamp a - way.

D.S. % al Coda

Coda

Elec. Gtr. 1

I looked a - round, a lous - y can - dle's all I found. Well,

Double time (♩ = 216)

Interlude:

w/Rhy. Fig. 3 *(Elec. Gtr. 1)*
4 times

w/bkgd. noise & fdbk.

Play 51 times

Elec. Gtr. 2

Rhy. Fig. 3

w/slide

D.S. % and fade

PROUD MARY

Words and Music by
J. C. FOGERTY

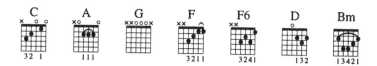

Moderately ♩ = 126
Intro:

1. Left a good job __ in the cit - y,
2. 3. *See additional lyrics*

work - in' for the man __ ev - 'ry night and day __ and I nev - er lost __ one min -

- ute of sleep - in', wor - ry - in' 'bout the way __ things might have been. __

Chorus:

Big wheel a-keep on turn - in', Proud __ Mar - y keep on burn - in', roll -

Proud Mary – 3 – 1

122

Proud Mary – 3 – 2

Verse 2:
Cleaned a lot of plates in Memphis,
Pumped a lot of pain down in New Orleans.
But I never saw the good side of the city
Till I hitched a ride on a river boat queen.
(To Chorus:)

Verse 3:
If you come down to the river,
Bet you're gonna find some people who live.
You don't have to worry
'Cause you have no money,
People on the river are happy to give.
(To Chorus:)

SAN FRANCISCO
(Be Sure to Wear Some Flowers in Your Hair)

Words and Music by
JOHN PHILLIPS

THE NIGHT THEY DROVE OLD DIXIE DOWN

Robertson played fingerpicking-style backup acoustic guitar on this, the Band's most well-known song. It first appeared on "The Band" album, and was later a hit for Joan Baez. It has also been recorded by Merl Saunders, Tanya Tucker and others.

By
ROBBIE ROBERTSON

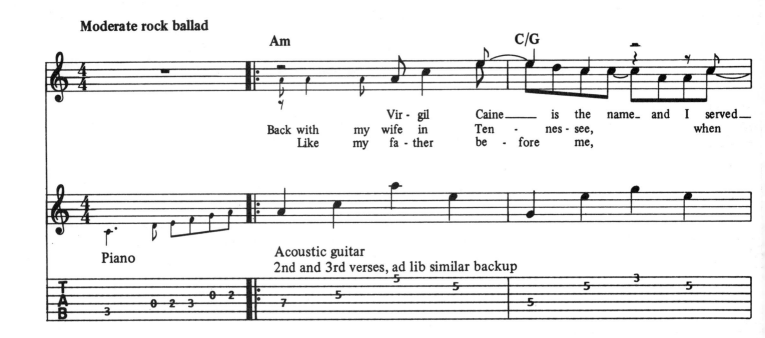

The Night They Drove Old Dixie Down - 5 - 1

127

The Night They Drove Old Dixie Down - 5 - 2

The Night They Drove Old Dixie Down - 5 - 3

The Night They Drove Old Dixie Down - 5 - 4

130

SEA OF JOY

Words and Music by
STEVE WINWOOD

Sea of Joy - 9 - 1

132

Sea of Joy - 9 - 2

134

Sea of Joy - 9 - 4

136

Sea of Joy - 9 - 6

Sea___ of___ joy._____

SOCIETY'S CHILD
(a/k/a "Society's Child (Baby I've Been Thinking")

Words and Music by
JANIS IAN

All gtrs. capo III

Moderately fast ♩ = 106

Intro:

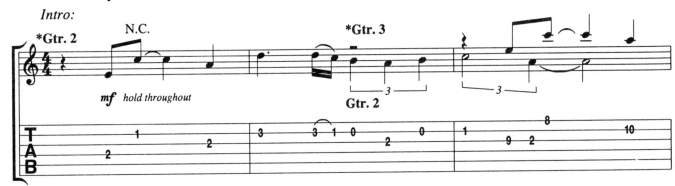

mf hold throughout

*Harpsichord arranged for two gtrs.

Society's Child – 3 – 1

142

Slower ♩ = 94

Chorus:

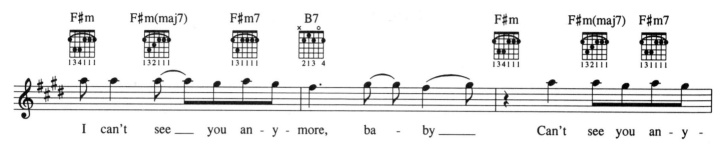

I can't see ___ you an-y-more, ba - by ___ Can't see you an-y-

1.2. more. **3.** more. ___ No, *Outro:* I don't wan-na see you an-y-

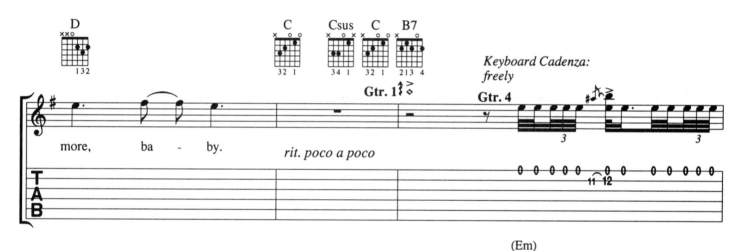

more, ba - by. *rit. poco a poco* *Keyboard Cadenza: freely*

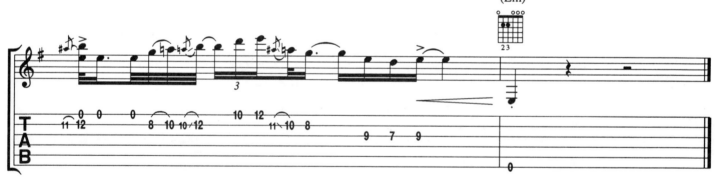

Verse 2:
Walk me down to school, baby
Everybody's acting deaf and blind
Until they turn and say
"Why don't you stick to your own kind?"
My teachers all laugh, their smirking stares
Cutting deep down in our affairs
Preachers of equality
Think they believe it
Then why won't they just let us be?
(To Chorus:)

Verse 3:
One of these days I'm gonna stop my listening
Gonna raise my head up high
One of these days I'm gonna
Raise up my glistening wings and fly.
But that day will have to wait for a while,
Baby, I'm only society's child
When we're older, things may change
But for now this is the way they must remain.
(To Chorus:)

TURN TURN TURN
(To Everything There Is a Season)

Words from the
Book of Ecclesiastes
Adaptation and Music by
PETE SEEGER

Moderately ♩ = 124

Intro:

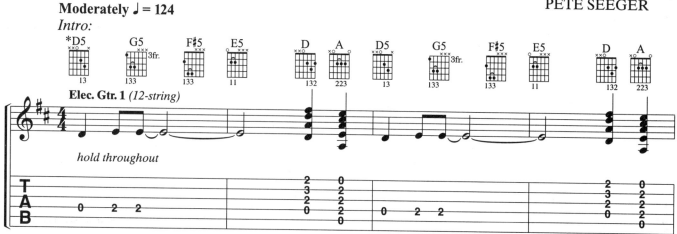

*Chords derived from overall harmony.

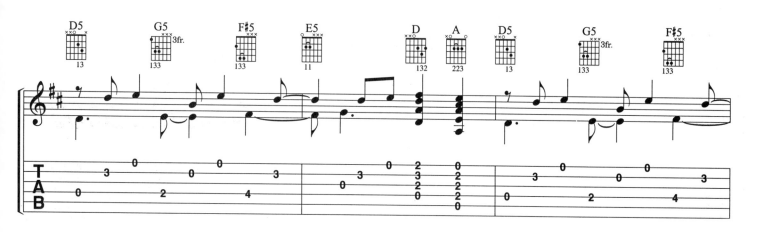

𝄋 *Chorus:*

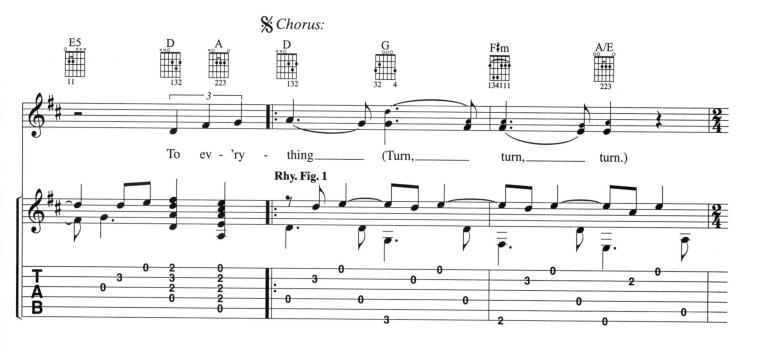

To ev-'ry-thing____ (Turn,_____ turn,_____ turn.)

Rhy. Fig. 1

144

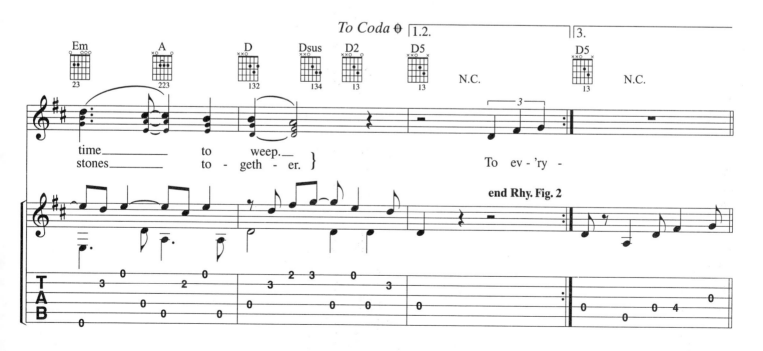

Turn Turn Turn - 5 - 3

146

Guitar Solo:

Coda

D5

Elec. Gtr. 1

N.C.

Outro:

D5   G5   F#5   E5   D   A

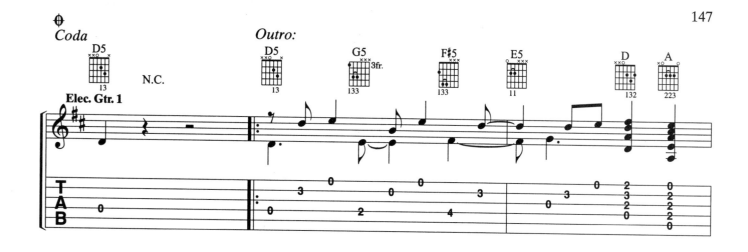

Repeat and fade

D5   G5   F#5   E5   D   A

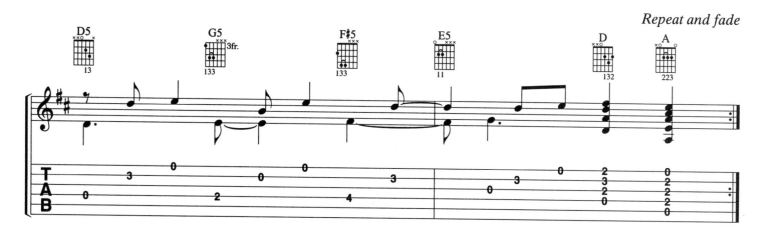

Verse 3:
A time of love, a time of hate.
A time of war, a time of peace.
A time you may embrace,
A time to refrain from embracing.
(To Guitar Solo:)

Verse 4:
A time to gain, a time to lose.
A time to rend, a time to sew.
A time for love, a time for hate.
A time for peace; I swear it's not too late.
(To Coda)

Turn Turn Turn - 5 - 5

STAGE FRIGHT

This is the title song from the "Stage Fright" recording, released in 1970. However, the frenetic, high-energy solo that concludes the transcription is from the 1976 "Last Waltz" concert recording.

By
ROBBIE ROBERTSON

Stage Fright - 4 - 1

150

Stage Fright - 4 - 3

Solo during vamp (live version)

SUGAR MAGNOLIA

Words by
ROBERT HUNTER and BOB WEIR

Music by
BOB WEIR

1. Sug - ar Mag - no - lia, blos-soms bloom - ing, heads all emp - ty and I ____

2. - 4. *See additional lyrics*

Rhy. Fig. 1 *(Both gtrs.)*

156

Coda 2

Verse 5:

Uh, some-times _ when the cuck - oo's cry - ing,   when the moon _ is half -

- way _ down, _   some - times _ when the night is _ dy - ing,

Oo. _

I take me out _ and I wan - der a - round. _

I wan - der 'round. _

Ah. _

Sugar Magnolia - 6 - 5

Outro:

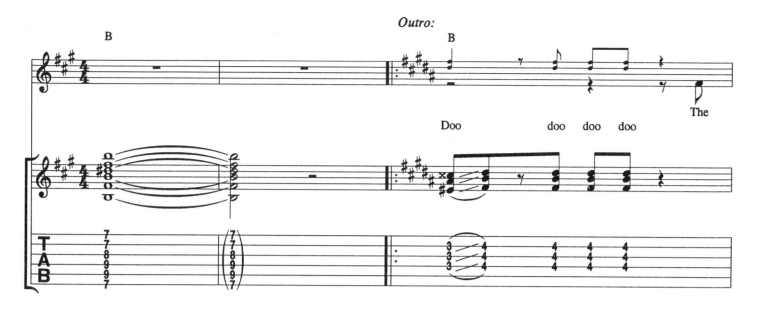

*Repeat & fade

*Lead vocal ad lib.
on repeats.

Verse 2:
Sweet blossom, come on under the willow,
We can have high times if you abide.
We can discover the wonders of nature,
Rolling in the rushes, down by the riverside.
(To Bridge:)

Verse 3:
Well, she comes skimmin' through rays of violet,
She can wade in a drop of dew.
She don't come and I don't follow,
Waits backstage while I sing to you.

Verse 4:
Well, she can dance a Cajun rhythm,
Jump like a Willys in four - wheel - drive.
She's a summer love in the spring, fall and winter.
She can make happy any man alive.
(To Chorus:)

Bridge 2:
She's got everything delightful,
She's got everything I need.
A breeze in the pines, and the summer moonlight,
Crazy in the sunlight, yes indeed.
(To Coda 2:)

SUNSHINE OF YOUR LOVE

Words and Music by
JACK BRUCE, PETE BROWN
and ERIC CLAPTON

Sunshine of Your Love - 6 - 1

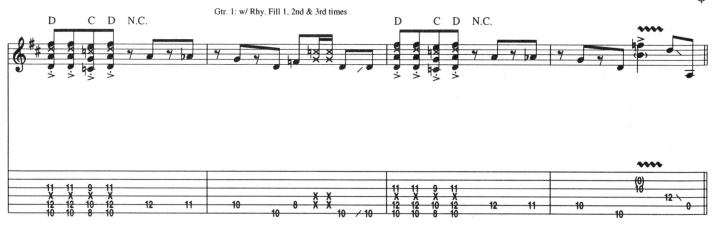

Chorus

I've _ been wait - ing so _ long to _ be where _ I'm go - ing

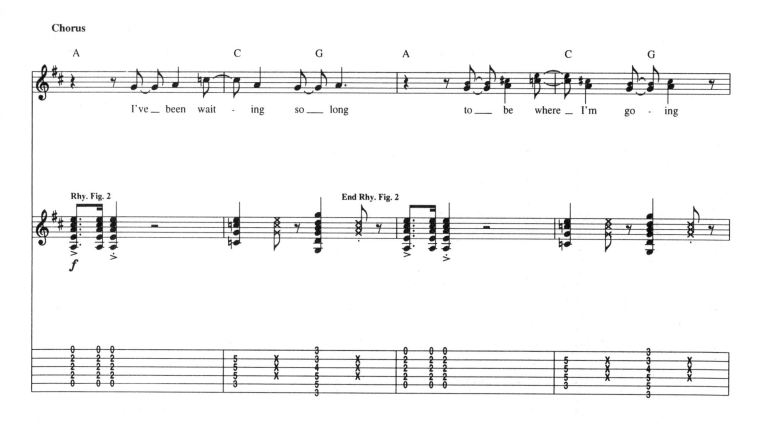

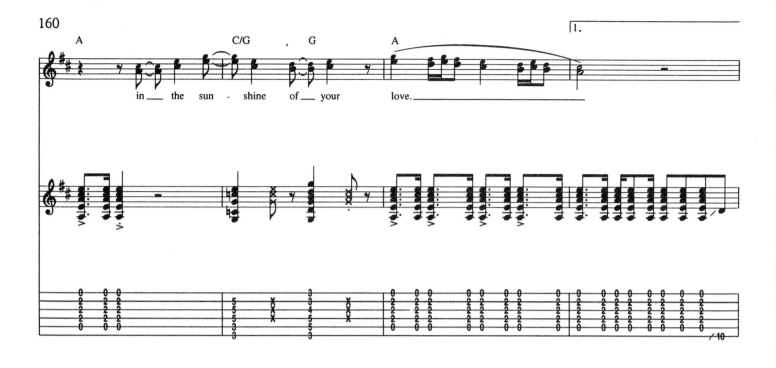

in __ the sun - shine of __ your love. _____

2. I'm __

Guitar Solo

Gtr. 2 (dist.)

Gtr. 1

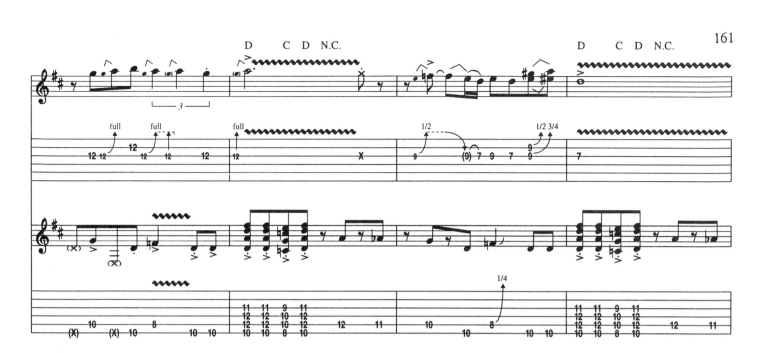

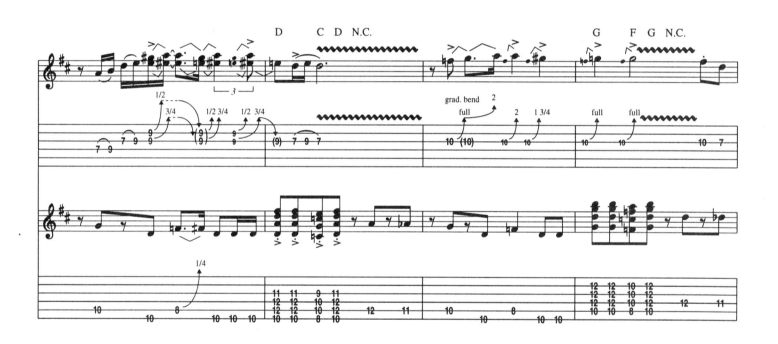

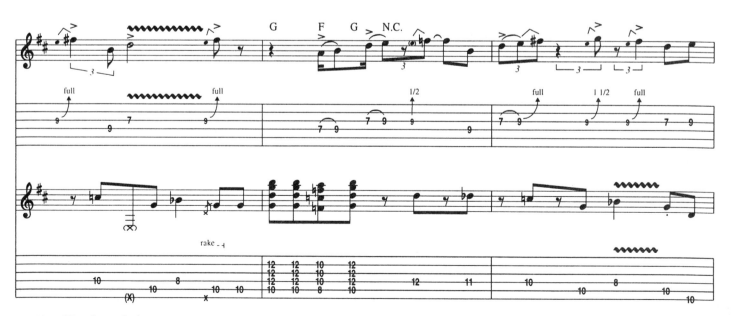

162

D.S. al Coda
(2nd lyrics)

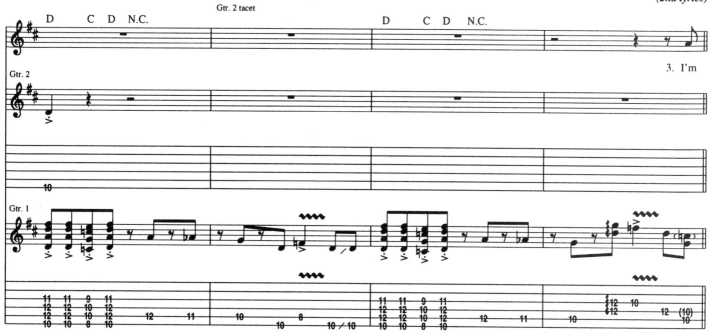

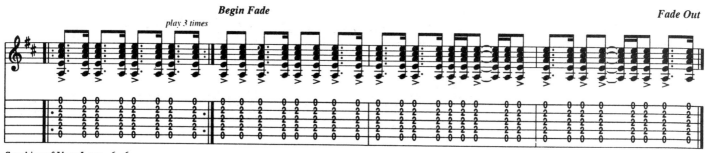

Sunshine of Your Love - 6 - 6

TUPELO HONEY

Words and Music by
VAN MORRISON

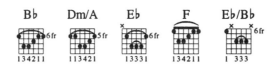

Tupelo Honey – 4 – 2

166

Verses 2 & 3:
You can't stop us
On the road to freedom.
You can't stop us
'Cause our eyes can see.
Men with insight,
Men of granite,
Knights in armor intent on chivalry.
(To Chorus:)

UNCLE JOHN'S BAND

Words by
ROBERT HUNTER

Music by
JERRY GARCIA

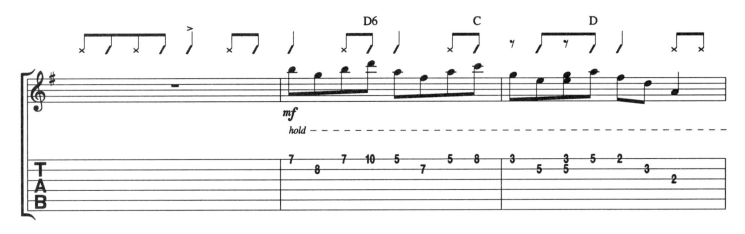

1. Well, the first days _ are _ the

2. - 4. *See additional lyrics*

Uncle John's Band - 5 - 1

169

Uncle John's Band - 5 - 2

Got some things to talk __ a - bout __ here __ be-side the __ ris-

-ing __ tide. __ Come hear __ Un - cle John's Band __

play - ing to the tide. __ Come on a - long or go __

__ a - lone, __ he's __ come to take his chil - dren home.

Gtr. 1
Gtr. 2

Play 7 times

hold - - - - - - - - - - - - -

Wo __ oh, __ what I __ want to know: __

172

Verse 2 :
It's a buck dancer's choice my friends;
Better take my advice.
You know all the rules by now
And the fire from the ice.
Will you come with me?
Won't you come with me?
Woah oh, what I want to know:
Will you come with me?
(To Guitar Solo:)

Verse 3 :
It's the same story the crow told me,
It's the only one he knows.
Like the morning sun you come
And like the wind you go.
Ain't no time to hate;
Barely time to wait
Woah oh, what I want to know:
Where does the time go?

Verse 4 :
I live in a silver mine
And I call it Beggars Tomb.
I got me a violin
And I beg you call the tune.
Anybody's choice,
I can hear your voice.
No oh, what I want to know:
How does the song go?
(To Chorus :)

Uncle John's Band - 5 - 5

UNFAITHFUL SERVANT

Yet another tune from "The Band" album, *UNFAITHFUL SERVANT* featured a fine, acoustic, bluesy solo played against pretty, almost majestic chord changes. The additional solo, played on electric guitar, is from The Band's 1972 "live" concert recording, "Rock of Ages." Here, Robertson displayed some trademark "pick harmonics." The song, like many Band tunes, has a startlingly unusual lyric. What other rock band could write and sing from the point of view of a "master" bidding goodbye to the servant with whom he's had an affair? (The Rolling Stones could do it, but it would be snide instead of wistful!)

By
ROBBIE ROBERTSON

Unfaithful Servant - 5 - 1

174

Unfaithful Servant - 5 - 2

A WHITER SHADE OF PALE

Words and Music by
KEITH REID and GARY BROOKER

A Whiter Shade of Pale - 2 - 2

WOODSTOCK

Words and Music by
JONI MITCHELL

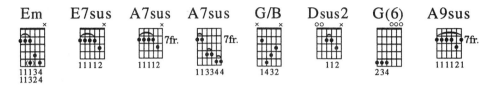

Tune Gtr. 1 down:

⑥ = D♭   ③ = G♭
⑤ = A♭   ② = B♭
④ = D♭   ① = E♭

Freely
Intro:

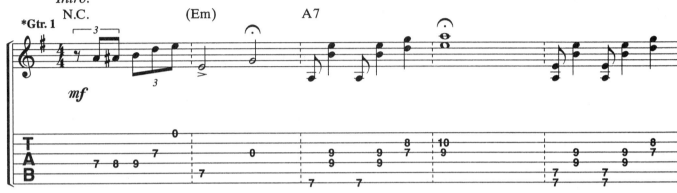

*Electric piano arranged for gtr.

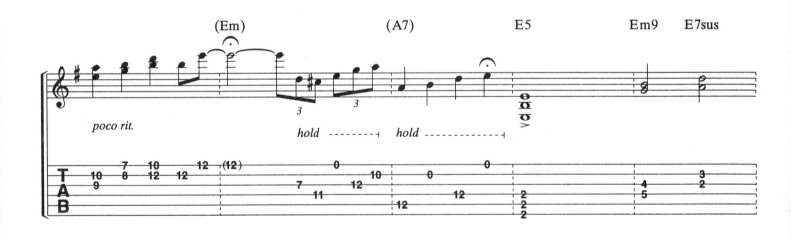

Moderately ♩ = ca. 108

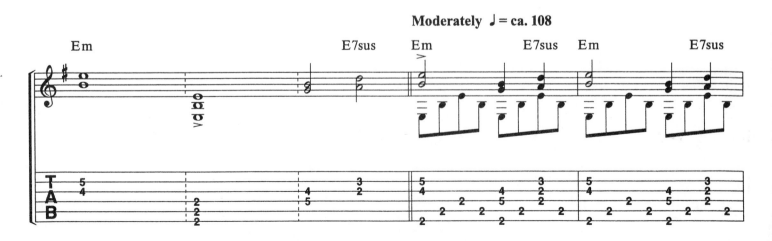

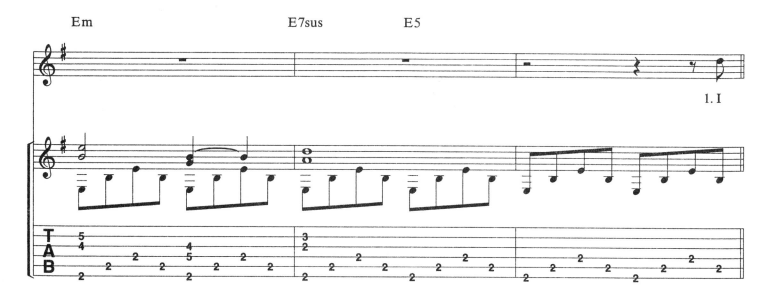

Woodstock - 9 - 2

182

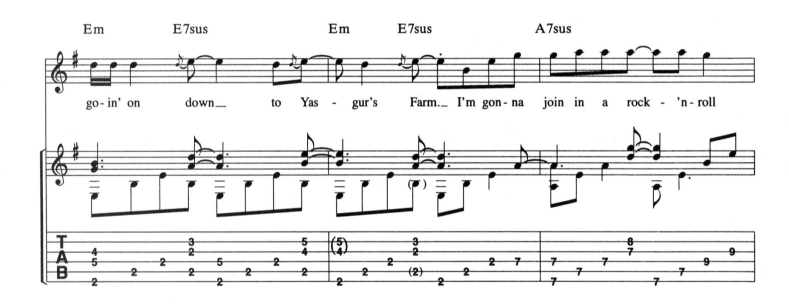

Woodstock - 9 - 3

gar - den.

Bkgd. vcl.: Doo, doo,   doo, doo, doo, doo, doo,

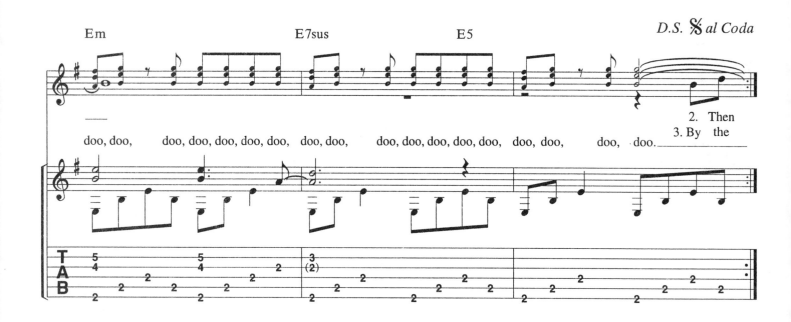

doo, doo,   doo, doo, doo, doo, doo,   doo, doo,   doo, doo, doo, doo, doo,   doo, doo,   doo, doo.

D.S. 𝄋 al Coda

2. Then
3. By the

Coda

bove_ our_____ na - tion._____ We are

Chorus:

star - dust,_____ bil - lion year_____ old___ car -

- bon. We are gold - en,

caught in the dev - il's bar - gain, and we got to___ get___ our -

selves   back   to   the   gar   -

- den.

rit. poco a poco

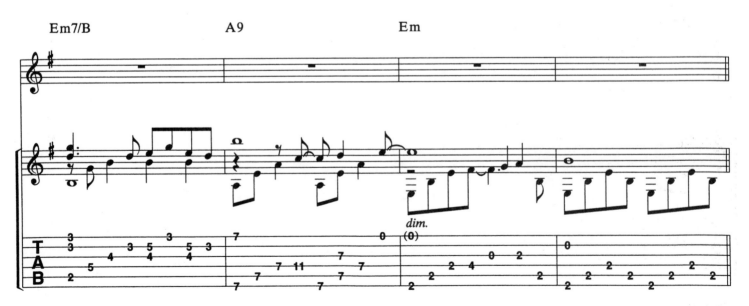

dim.

Slower
Outro:

Woodstock - 9 - 8

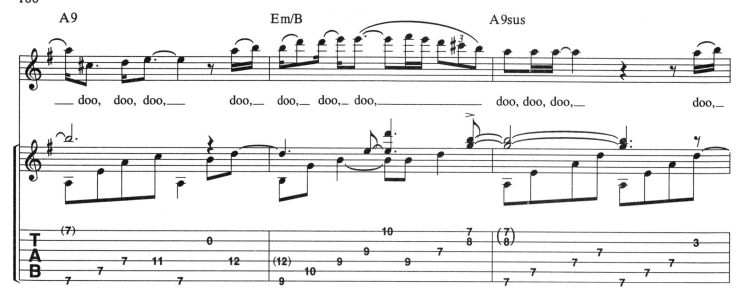

*Left-hand tap.
**Right-hand tap.

Verse 2:

Then can I walk beside you?
I have come here to lose the smog.
And I feel to be a cog
In something turning.
Well, maybe it is just the time of year,
Or maybe it's the time of man.
I don't know who I am,
But, you know, life is for learning.
(To Chorus:)

Verse 3:

By the time we got to Woodstock,
We were half a million strong,
And everywhere was song and celebration.
And I dreamed I saw the bombers
Riding shotgun in the sky,
And they were turning into butterflies
Above our nation.

WORDS OF LOVE

Words and Music by
JOHN PHILLIPS

Words of love,_ so soft and ten - der, won't win a girl's heart_ an - y - more._
2nd time (now.)

If you love_ her, then you___ must send_ her some - where where she's_ nev - er

been be - fore._ Worn out phras - es and long - ing gaz - es won't
(Ooh, ooh,____

get you where you want to go. Words of love,_
ooh, ooh.____) (Ooh,

soft and ten - der, won't___ win her.___
ooh, ooh.____)

Words of Love - 3 - 1

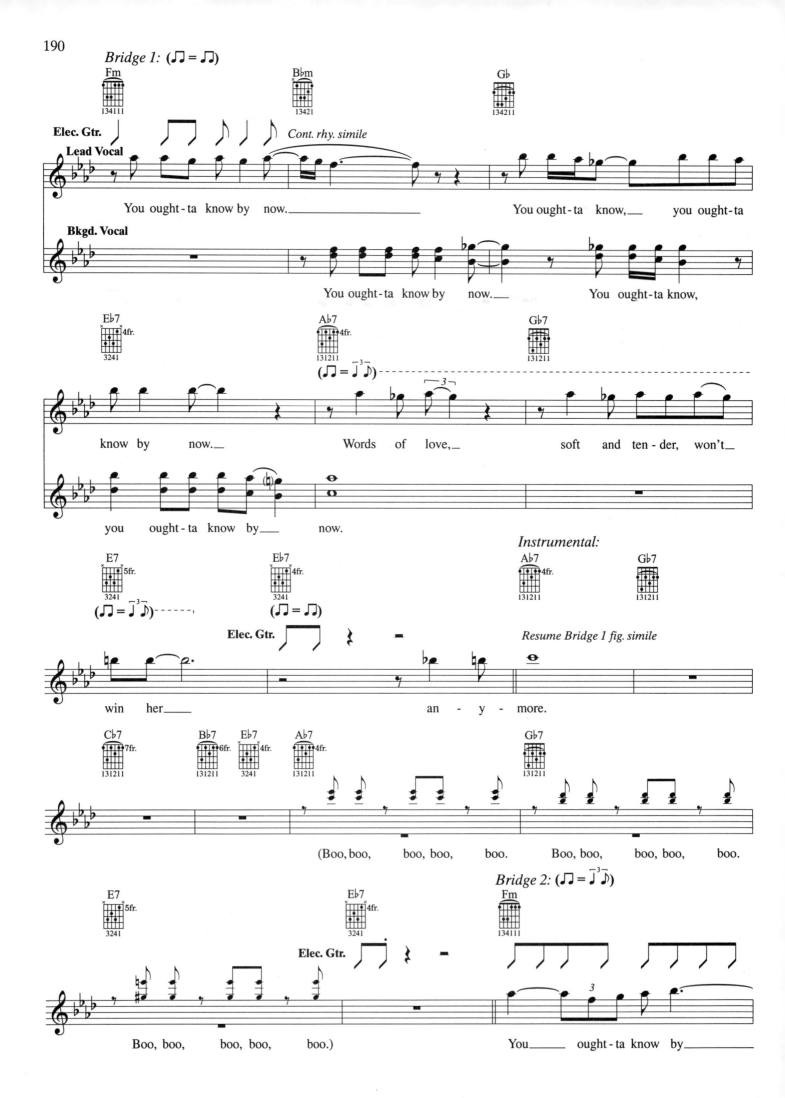

GUITAR TAB GLOSSARY **

TABLATURE EXPLANATION

READING TABLATURE: Tablature illustrates the six strings of the guitar. Notes and chords are indicated by the placement of fret numbers on a given string(s).

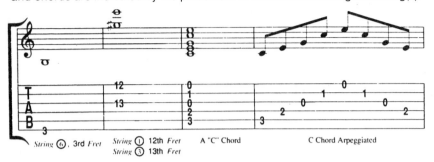

String ⑥, 3rd Fret   String ① 12th Fret   A "C" Chord   C Chord Arpeggiated
                      String ③ 13th Fret

BENDING NOTES

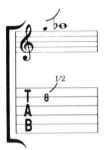

HALF STEP: Play the note and bend string one half step.*

PREBEND AND RELEASE: Bend the string, play it, then release to the original note.

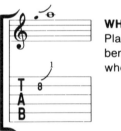

WHOLE STEP: Play the note and bend string one whole step.

RHYTHM SLASHES

STRUM INDICATIONS: Strum with indicated rhythm. The chord voicings are found on the first page of the transcription underneath the song title.

INDICATING SINGLE NOTES USING RHYTHM SLASHES: Very often single notes are incorporated into a rhythm part. The note name is indicated above the rhythm slash with a fret number and a string indication.

*A half step is the smallest interval in Western music; it is equal to one fret. A whole step equals two frets.

**By Kenn Chipkin and Aaron Stang

ARTICULATIONS

HAMMER ON: Play lower note, then "hammer on" to higher note with another finger. Only the first note is attacked.

PULL OFF: Play higher note, then "pull off" to lower note with another finger. Only the first note is attacked.

LEGATO SLIDE: Play note and slide to the following note. (Only first note is attacked).

PALM MUTE: The note or notes are muted by the palm of the pick hand by lightly touching the string(s) near the bridge.

ACCENT: Notes or chords are to be played with added emphasis.

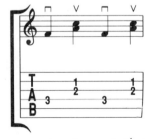

DOWN STROKES AND UPSTROKES: Notes or chords are to be played with either a downstroke (⊓·) or upstroke (∨) of the pick.